Committing Patriotism

Non-Violent Strategies for U.S. Citizens to Regain Their Government
(Revised and updated for 2026)

By

Brad Havens

Cover Art By

Brad Havens

Photography By

Shaun Armendariz

WWW.MOUNTAINFIREMEDIA.COM

ISBN# 978-1-79477-650-0

TABLE OF CONTENTS

INTRODUCTION

Let's face it. The Bastards won. They abused our Trust, and took our Country from us while we were being told to go shopping. Fortunately for us, we still have enough of this thing called a Constitution, which - when we choose to exercise it - prevents these Big Money Bastards from hanging on to what they stole for very long.

But we haven't exercised it in a long, long time - we've been too distracted - and they've been doing their best to keep us that way using a lot of fearmongering, fomenting Anger and Hatred. Once again, fortunately for us, we don't have to play their game to beat them. We already have a game they have to play with us, and we can change the rules in our favor without ever having to resort to violence or drastic, Bloody Revolution.

We've been convinced over the years that we have to keep playing their game, and they keep changing the rules in their favor whenever we do. But that's not how our Government is set up. In reality, when you step into the United States, it's our game. And it's our rules to play. That's what the Constitution guarantees, and that's why Bankers and Businessmen - the real Enemy - hate our Freedoms. That's why they've been trying to convince you that the Constitution is "quaint" and irrelevant, when it is exactly the necessary tool to defeat them.

So, if you're game, here are some new rules for those Bastards who stole the D.C. Beltway from Us, including a few proposed Amendments to our Constitution to bolster our Inalienable Rights & make sure our "Representatives" don't have another memory lapse regarding their oaths, or forget who they work for, either. All it takes is organization & a commitment to demand that our Representatives unseat the Billionaires and end the Corporate Oligarchy.

No bullets necessary.

EMBRACING & EMPOWERING
THE REAL "FOURTH BRANCH"

It has been said that our News Organizations and the Journalists reporting on activities in Government represent a de facto "Fourth Branch" of Government after the Executive, Legislative & Judicial Branches established by the Constitution. Apparently, this title is deemed appropriate because of the scrutiny "the Press" allegedly subjects our "Representatives" and political policies to when researching and reporting stories they present to the public.

However, if this past election year (2016) is any indication, with the many examples of candidate favoritism and an overall absence of objective reporting, it has been made abundantly clear that our "news organizations" have become functionary mouthpieces for supporting political agendas, as well as the agendas of their corporate sponsors. One need only query "DAPL" in a search engine to observe the astonishing lack of attention "Mainstream Media" paid to a story that, at its core, is about an Oil Company refusing to comply with Federal Law, and instead, enlisting out-of-state law enforcement officers (from upwards of 5 different states at one point) to commit acts of violence (e.g. sacred burial grounds were desecrated in a deliberate act of intimidation) & unwarranted arrests against an unarmed populace attempting to protect a major water supply.

Further, our seated President was aware of these events and yet allowed these things to happen. Ignoring High Crimes that include election tampering, corporate theft, and a President abdicating his legal responsibilities to his own Citizens? THAT is a blatant failure of Big Media and "objective" news reporting. Whatever pretense may have existed, there is no other conclusion than Big Media in its current form is compromised and incapable of presenting objective information to the People. It is impossible for a tool to govern men. It cannot serve as any "Branch" of Government; it can only be directed by those it serves, and it must serve the People.

The true "Fourth Branch" of our Government, unspecified but wholly acknowledged and empowered by our Constitution, is comprised of the Citizens of the United States themselves. The fact that we have abdicated that responsibility to others, and allowed ourselves to be subjugated for so many years, does not change the fact that we are not subjects of our Government. Our Government, as provided by our Constitution, is subject to the Will of People of the United States. No Corporation, no outside Government, no Political Party within our own Government is granted any powers of government that supersedes the consensus of the People.

NO MATTER WHAT THEY TELL YOU.

CITIZEN'S INTERVENTION

"...That whenever any form of government becomes destructive of these ends it is the Right of the People to alter or abolish it, and to institute new government, laying its foundations on such principles and organizing its powers in such form as to them shall seem most likely to effect their Safety and Happiness."
                    -U.S. Declaration of Independence, July 4th, 1776

Okay. This is the Truth. Here's the real situation, and no matter what you think of it, there is only one way out of it. No more anger, no more outbursts or name-calling. I don't care what color you are or what's between you legs. I really don't care what god you pray to, as long as you're not using that as an excuse to force your opinion on someone else - we need real progress for our families & our future here on this earth, not hope for a promised land in some "afterlife". We can all do this together. We have to do it together, or it will fail. And they know it.

But if we do come together - if we do succeed - in so doing, not only will "We the People" of the United States be putting ourselves on a path towards regaining control of our own proper, Constitutionally mandated & guaranteed Representative Government, we will be demonstrating to the World that we can be responsible for ourselves and give these War Criminals a taste of some good old fashioned American Justice.

We can thank our current President, if for no other reason, for being the electric prod that woke the People - made us want to become active, ask questions, and take stock of our government again. The powers that be will say it's too late - Hell, maybe it is too late - but in this Information Age, we are more aware and more capable than ever before of taking back from those who coaxed our "Representatives" away from us. These "elite" who would actively work to undermine our Constitution and bankrupt our Nation and its People for nothing more than profit are the source of our corruption.

Not nearly so anonymous as they used to be, between the panama papers, wikileaks, the podesta emails, and on and on, we have many legal, non-violent options available to do what's right for all of us. And we don't have to wait for any damn elections, either.

So, what follows are some very carefully measured, Constitutionally legal and appropriate options for U.S. Citizens to consider in terms of reforms to our system of government with two goals in mind:

1) Taking financial influence out of politics entirely. Greed has irrevocably corrupted our system, so our system must be adapted to prevent this from ever occurring again.

2) Returning the political power base to the Citizenry and creating a Representative Government that more accurately reflects the Nation and its real Constituency.

It is the responsibility of U.S. Citizens to protect their Democracy. These proposals for new Amendments & revised Policies and Procedures create methods to accomplish exactly that. Again, we do not have to wait for elections - the organizations, the People, the devices to accomplish this are all readily available, they simply need to be assembled and put into action.

ELECTION REFORMS:
UPDATING THE DOG & PONY SHOW

Step 1: Return the Inalienable Right to Vote to the U.S. Citizen.

An immediate vote and ratification of two Amendments to the Constitution that guarantees every Citizen the Right to Vote - To wit:

 - **Amendment #28:** Congress shall pass no Law that prohibits any Citizen from exercising their Right to Vote in any City, State, or Federal election at any time, regardless of political party affiliation or membership status in any organization. Any Laws currently in place which deny the Right to Vote to any Citizen, or inhibit or alter the true accounting of the Popular Vote in any election as outlined above, under any circumstances, is hereby automatically and immediately rescinded. Any Religious Organization advocating for any politician or government policy will automatically lose its tax-exempt status.

 - **Amendment #29:** The Right to Vote for U.S. Representatives and Government Policies and Procedures remains exclusively for U.S. Citizens and will not apply to any Corporation, Business, Non-Profit, Religious or Legal Organization, or any manufactured, non-living, non-human entity. The designated Election Day will be an official Government Holiday where Citizens may be relieved of duty to exercise their Right to Vote without loss of compensation from their employer.

WHAT THESE TWO AMENDMENTS ACCOMPLISH: The Electoral College? Super Delegates? Corporate favoritism? Religious manipulation? Abolish all of that interference with these two Amendments. Same with Citizen's United, and any "Law" that was passed which ever inhibited the Right to Vote. Uninhibited 1st Amendment Freedom of Expression where it matters most: choosing your Representative and your Government.

Step 2: Standardize and Centralize the Electoral Process for every U.S. Citizen

We have to accept that the only way to return influence back to the People is to remove private money from the election process. There is only one way to remove private money from the election process, and that is to remove elections from private control.

We must take responsibility for our Vote, and ourselves. To do that, we must make our election process a Federally funded system with Civilian oversight. No lobbyists, no private fundraisers, no outside money. If we as U.S. Citizens want to own the elections, we have to pay for them ourselves. But, you know, we can be cheap about it - it's our election, not theirs.

Fortunately for us, when it comes to the requirements for such a task, a lot of the heavy lifting has already been done. While they may be loath to admit it, Facebook, Google, and Amazon, amongst others, have all had and/or currently maintain a relationship with the CIA or DARPA or some other Government entity. Simply put, they can claim Proprietary Rights all they want, but every aspect of data collection, video and IM communications, financial transactions - all of it was developed and implemented in whole or in part with some sort of Federal involvement. How else was it suddenly so easy for the NSA (or any government/IT hacker) to spy on you?

And as it happens, all of that is exactly what would be required to centralize the election process under one easily accessible, secured online database. It would simply take a little tweaking and fine tuning, making a few adjustments to platforms that are already active and readily adaptable to the cause. Whether they willingly joined or chose to be compelled, the tools and talent necessary to expedite this public service for our Country and its Citizens would be facilitated via these active, multi-billion online monopolies. And that's as far as their involvement would be allowed to go. Once the centralized site was ready for launch, all private Corporations & Contractors would be locked out of the system and prevented from any further influence or administration.

Accessibility and accountability are the core issues. As we have seen from Republican "Leaders" like Mitch McConnell, politicians will hide from their Constituency rather than face accountability for an unpopular decision. It is their Constitutional Obligation to be accessible to their public, and yet they refuse. Why? How are they allowed to get away with this negligence? Money. Billionaires and Bankers have turned our Representatives into hypocritical Cowards, fawning over whomever pays the most to keeping the mewling pigs grunting at the trough, ignoring their Oaths and ignoring the People.

To that end, not only would this proposed online platform simplify and secure the voting process for U.S. Citizens, it would also allow exclusive access to their Representatives in a social media style environment. So, on the heels of those two Amendments (#28 & #29) comes the following proposal outlining this concept for Internet-based reform to our election process:

A new social media site exclusive to U.S. Citizens, designed to keep them informed about politicians and policies in their state and at the Federal level, so that they can see what's happening, can vote & send emails, and are encouraged to remain active & engaged in the process of government beyond simply waiting for Election Day.

With this centralized, online platform, not only could you cast your vote in a secure environment, you would be able to engage with U.S. Citizens much like you would on Facebook or other sites where a Directory of Members would allow people to engage with each other. But more importantly, members could engage their Representatives in real time. Access to information regarding policies and bill negotiations would be available in real time so Citizens would know who was influencing their Representatives to act in a certain manner and why.

In total, this centralized site would provide three main functions:

1 - Control the Vote:

- One vote per Citizen, no vote without citizenship.

- Verified by social security number/naturalized ID "green card".

- Confirmation and time stamp receipt provided - proof your vote was counted!

- Able to follow in real time as Votes are made & counted nationwide.

- Physical Polling Places still open, but interface is the same for everyone.

- Mail-In votes available, but election forms still require SS# verification & online template format. Early online voting would be encouraged as an alternative to mail-in voting.

2 - Access to Politicians and the Policies they Create:

-Enhanced "reality style" programming to present background information about our Representatives and their Policies to really make it more of an interactive "Behind the Curtain" forum than the passive show it is today.

- Presentations regarding local, state & federal activities & proposals - who was doing what, where - would be centralized and made available for reference to help oversee political maneuvering at every level and stage of government.

- The House and Senate would be required to submit "State of the Union" reports bi-annually, via this centralized forum, to justify their existence and prove their adherence to the Constitution.

- Politicians, Candidates & Citizens could initiate topics for discussion/ vote in forums.

- Candidates & current Politicians would be required to engage in forums and post updates about their activities and answer questions.

- Candidates would be required to conduct all of their campaigning, with the only exception being personal appearances, through this site.

- Candidates would be required to debate each other through this site, simulcast on Networks & archived for future reference.

- Any meetings with Corporate Lobbyists attempting to affect policy would be made public to be openly discussed in forums.

- An easily accessible "Lobby List" would be maintained to track attempts by Corporations, etc. to negatively influence policy in their favor.

3 - Access to Each Other:

- Members would be encouraged to participate in forums, organize local groups, organize petitions & stay active in their Representative's activities. It would be like a fantasy football league, only a real opportunity to organize with real results affecting Government Players and Policy.

- All topics required to be politically or government based - no celebrity gossip, no religious content, no sports updates or reviews, nor any of those misleading & deliberately provocative memes - the intent of this site will be to encourage real civic action, not to simply complain about the world.

- Whistleblowers come forward! Be heard! Help make Partisanship take a backseat to Progress. As we see on a daily basis these days, policy decisions are not made for the benefit of the People, and the People always suffer for it. As part of membership, no Citizen will be required to declare any party affiliation. In fact, such party loyalties would be discouraged as a

potential detriment to the First Amendment and the Bill of
Rights.

How do we pay for all of this? According to the latest numbers
(from 2016), the United States outspends the next seven
Countries combined by $100Billion on maintaining its illegal
wars overseas. By ending the illegal "War on Terror" and cutting
the budget for military operations by half, not only would the
U.S. continue to outspend our next closer competitor (China) by
more then $100Billion, we would be freeing up $375Billion for
investment in infrastructure and many other badly needed
services. ***

By my guess, implementing this proposed website and gaining
control of the Vote would cost about a tenth of what would result
from cutting the military budget in half, leaving well over
$300Billion for Citizens to determine where to invest - Health
Care? Absolve Student Debt? College Grants? Alternative
Energy Development? Cleaning up the Oceans? Those would all
be great subjects for the forums.

New job opportunities, new economic strategies, engagement of
social classes regardless of income - the Majority would decide in
all cases. From there it would be the responsibility of the
Representatives to get it done in Congress.

For the first time in History, Citizens would decide the allocation
of Government Resources, not Corporations or megalomaniacal
Tyrants.

***In 2026, I now say that with the recent audits and exposure of
fraud and mishandled financing, in addition to trimming the
military budget, these resources would either be sent where they
were supposed to go, or redirected towards this service model.

Step 3: The Voter and Elections Protections Department

That website is pretty ambitious - who would run it and how would it operate? Well, as the site would be the principal online interface between Citizens and Government, there would have to be a Department designated to oversee implementation and operation. The specific mission of this Department would be to provide oversight and detailed reporting on candidates, election-related events, and election-related proposals throughout the entire process of campaigning to ensure open, transparent, unhindered elections. It would also maintain the community forums and guidelines. Two independent organizations working within this Department would need to be established to oversee and provide transparency throughout the entire voting process:

- Citizen's Election Oversight Committee

Responsible for testing, approving or denying voting machines and online systems designed exclusively for capturing and recording an accurate ballot. Also responsible for ensuring Citizens have all information required to make an informed decision prior to casting their vote, and a proof copy of their ballot for their records.

- Citizens will be allowed one vote, directly tied to their Social Security/Naturalized ID number ensuring one vote per U.S. Citizen. Outside (vetted) observers would oversee election polling places and online vote count so that no political party, private investor, or individual politician has influence on the vote count - They can all stay at home and watch it in real time with the rest of us.

- Vote can be cast in person, or via secure online server. "Mail-In" voting will be provided via downloadable app, secured to ensure the vote is received and counted as intended by the Citizen preferring to mail in their vote.

- If the Citizen declines to Vote, they will be requested to mark "Decline" on their Ballot - this is the best and only way to guarantee that every vote matters, is counted, and Citizens may vote their conscience.

-The voting process will be operated by Federal Custodians, but overseen by an independent, vetted Civilian Voting Officers to ensure accuracy of the vote counts.

- Federal Election Management Department

The function of this Department is two-fold:

First, to centralize all election activity - funding, hiring, resources, etc. - into one wholly transparent bureaucracy with the sole charter of providing U.S. Citizens fair, objective, uniform Elections. Corporations, Private Investors, Independent Financiers of any sort would not be allowed to participate in funding, advertising, promoting, campaigning or otherwise interfering with the election process whatsoever. There would be no need for any outside influence on election campaign funding, or the candidates themselves, as all of that will be provided in an open, transparent manner via the Federal Election Management Department.

Broadcast networks would be required to provide equal time and coverage to each candidate - none of this paid punditry smear campaign shit - only real facts about the candidates and their views. No more "accidentally" donating $5Billion worth of airtime to a favored candidate. And since they've proven they can afford such generosity, Broadcast Networks would provide this equal time and coverage at no cost as part of their contribution to civil service, providing US Citizens objective information to make an informed decision.

A natural result of this Charter is the prevention of lobbying, outside investment, corporate favoritism, or any other term for buying a candidate with campaign contributions or broadcast time or any other incentive that might lead a politician away from their obligations to serve the People.

Further:

- Corporations would not be allowed to donate to, or advocate for, any candidates using company resources or employee time, they could only say what their business would do to remain relevant to the local community/state/nation. Business Owners and Executives would not be allowed to campaign for specific Candidates or Policies within the workplace - the Individual Right to Privacy, as well as Freedom of Expression and the Right to Vote would not be infringed without some financial penalty to the Executive attempting to exploit their position.

- Any financial contribution or "gift" from a Corporation, Executive or Business Owner would be immediately investigated for attempted bribery.

Second, this Department would to be responsible for the actual collection, processing, and counting of the votes. The counting would be public, video recorded for potential review, and witnessed and confirmed by designated members of the Citizen's Election Oversight Committee. Any disparity between exit polls and actual counts would be automatically reviewed. Any discrepancies in the vote count could be addressed with a re-count, having Citizens provide their proof of voting, or simply re-voting.

The bottom line is, we have the tech to handle financial transactions securely, maintain multiple video & IM communications in real time, and maintain online communities specifically to help organize political groups and activities. We have no excuse not to implement these tools into a cohesive, centralized, secure database that accomplishes our needs as Citizens while simultaneously shutting down the powers of corruption from the greatest threat to our Constitution - the Billionaires, Bankers, and Business Owners.

You know what's "quaint" and old fashioned?

Believing that money makes you better than any other person. It doesn't. In most cases, it does just the opposite.

The Constitution is still the most progressive Legal Doctrine ever written. As Citizens of the United States, we can affect change. Real change. And we do not have to wait for an election year. United in one voice, our Government has to listen, or it no longer becomes the legal government of the land. That is our Right as guaranteed by the Declaration of Independence and our Constitution.

A Citizen's Intervention would make it clear to those addicted to power in D.C. that we still have the authority to take the car keys away from a drunk driver.

ELECTION REFORMS FOR
THE HOUSE OF REPRESENTATIVES

"All legislative Powers herein granted shall be vested in a Congress of the United States, which shall consist of a Senate and House of Representatives."

> -- Article 1, Section 1, U.S. Constitution

"No Person shall be a Representative who shall not have attained to the Age of twenty five Years, and been seven Years a Citizen of the United States, and who shall not, when elected, be an Inhabitant of that State in which he shall be chosen."

> -- Article 1, Section 2, U.S. Constitution

"No Person shall be a Senator who shall not have attained to the Age of thirty five Years, and been nine Years a Citizen of the United States, and who shall not, when elected, be an Inhabitant of that State for which he shall be chosen."

> -- Article 1, Section 3, U.S. Constitution

Notice that nowhere does it say you have to be a lawyer, politician, or soldier to know a damn thing about doing the job. Know the Constitution and do your best by your Country for your fellow Americans. That is all that is required of you.

The stranglehold Lawyers have placed on our Legislative Branch has prevented U.S. Citizens from any hope of a genuine representative governance. By preventing lawyers and organized legal teams within the two Houses from unifying to stall the function of government, or undermine the Constitution, we would finally be able to see real Representative Government in action, and present issues which matter to Citizens, not Corporations.

"B-But... we need experienced 'leaders' to handle sensitive issues!" is the most common argument, to which I say: After 19 years (now 26years) of getting reamed by these guys, you really think we can't do any better for ourselves? You really want to keep lying, thieving, worthless "Leaders" like these in office? Come on, get Brave again!

- Amendment to Article 1, Section 1 - The first round of Candidates for Representatives of the Legislative Branch would be assigned by lottery according to population density - no campaigning, no gerrymandering, no districts, no exclusivity on profession - any able U.S. Citizen with a SS/Naturalized ID # could be selected. Once selected, all campaigning and debates would be run through the website with oversight provided by the two Election Protection Departments. Only two final Candidates per available position, in addition to the Incumbent when appropriate, and three public debates between them - other journalistic reports & interviews would provide relevant information about the Candidates prior to the Vote.

- Amendment to Article 1, Section 2 - The House of Representatives of the Legislative Branch would be restricted to a maximum of three 2-year terms.

- Amendment to Article 1, Section 3 - The Senate of the Legislative Branch would be restricted to one 6-year term.

- Amendment #30 - Representatives from each Branch of Government will be subject to an annual audit of government and personal finances to ensure their Constituents and Oaths of Office remain their first priority.

With this new approach to the election process, the need for constant fundraising is removed, providing more time for the individual Representative to actually commit to their Congressional responsibilities, engage with their Constituents, and concentrate on passing effective Laws that benefit the Majority as well as the Nation.

ELECTION REFORMS FOR
THE OFFICE OF THE PRESIDENT

"No Person except a natural born Citizen, or a Citizen of the United States, at the time of the Adoption of this Constitution, shall be eligible to the Office of President; neither shall any Person be eligible to that Office who shall not have attained to the Age of thirty five Years, and been fourteen Years a Resident within the United States"

-- Article 1, Section 1, U.S. Constitution

Notice that nowhere is there a requirement for a political party affiliation, gender, ethnicity, religious belief - not even a family name.

Under the proposed reforms, the Election of the Office of the President would vary slightly from the Elections for the House and Senate; however, the Office of the Vice President would be selected in the same manner, and the functions would not change.

- Amendments to Article 2, Section 1: The Election for the Office of the President would become a two-year cycle, beginning at the State level, managed primarily through the Election Website and partially subsidized by the Federal Election Management Department. It would provide any Citizen with the desire to run the opportunity to present themselves and petition for selection as their State's Candidate for Office of the President.

- After the first year of the election cycle, each state would have one duly elected candidate to represent their state for election. Then, the Federal Campaign Funding kicks in - An "Internal Campaign Budget" allotted to the final 50 Candidates - ensures that each Candidate receives the same amount of campaign support, exposure, and opportunity for debate at each stage of the election.

- The second year of the election cycle remains relatively the same, with significantly more debates and interviews and public vetting - a real opportunity to get to know the Candidates and their Policies well before the final ballot is cast - the Person elected to the Office of the President is chosen from the final two Candidates. The Incumbent could also run for a chance at a second term when appropriate.

- The most popular Candidate would win the Presidency, while the second most popular would take the seat of the Vice Presidency.

Not only does this method bring us closer to genuine Democracy, it absolutely destroys any need for partisan politics, a Two-Party System, or any of those easily corruptible influences that hinder a stable, beneficial government. By keeping the election process contained and transparent for all who participate, we can prevent any undue influence from sponsors, political parties, campaign contributions, paid pundits, or any of the traditional methods employed to prevent Citizens from real Representative Government.

With one properly managed, vetted, centralized website that allows U.S. Citizens access to their Representatives, as well as a secure method of voting, all the noise from Big Media - the "Political Experts", the SuperPAC (whatever) advertising, the overt propaganda - all of it would be relegated to where it belongs: the entertainment section.

The real source for honest, objective Government Accounting and Reporting would come from one secure outlet, administered by Federal employees, with oversight and approval from the Citizens themselves.

The way it should be.

FOREIGN POLICY REFORMS - ENDING THE WAR ON TERROR

It's actually pretty simple. Perpetual Warfare is an unsustainable diplomatic policy, and yet, it is our #1 Export to the World. We've withdrawn from Treaties and Trade Agreements, introduced Tariffs and Travel Bans, and turned building a Border Wall into a National Crisis. In the past two years, the United States has done its best to tell the World that it needs to do things our way, or else it faces Scorn, Sanctions, and Soldiers.

The World has responded in different ways. The European Union has openly declared that the United States can no longer be trusted. Russia and China have been working to build up trade in currencies other than the Dollar, uniting Asian and Eastern European Markets using a Gold Standard. Putin has already declared that the days of the U.S. Dollar dominating trade are over. He's quite confident, and why shouldn't he be? With the way Trump fawns over him and refuses to discuss what was done or said in those private meetings, it seems Putin may know more about the future of the United States better than Congress.

Effectively, the World has seen our cards and knows that we are bluffing. To pretend otherwise would be foolhardy and extremely shortsighted, unless the goal of the current Administration is to allow the devaluation of the Dollar as part of its isolationist policies. ***

The only way to avoid this inevitable conclusion is to reverse course on our contemporary military strategies - something that is impossible to accomplish under current conventional wisdom.

But, you gotta admit, it would be a surprising and welcome change in direction for the World to see the United States call truce, slash its military budget by half and re-invest that money helping to build a better planet for everyone.

Cutting the Military Budget by half would still allow for a formidable standing army capable of defending our borders from invasion – and still outspend the rest of the world while doing so.

That is all our Military should be required to do. A reallocation of funds for proper care for our wounded Vets, shelters for those in need, healthcare, education, alternative energies, and all those goodies other civilized nations can seem to afford only makes sense. By ending this War on Terror, revising and reducing all military operations & spending, and returning to a State of Diplomacy where the Bomb is not amongst the "first options on the table", the United States would initiate a means for other nations to stand down and follow suit, using the Art of Diplomacy instead of the blunt Cruelty of War.

The United States could remain a World Leader with a deliberate change of course towards peace - a specific Diplomatic Mission to abandon the bloody politics of Oil, and rectify the horrific consequences of War with a concerted effort to nurture peace, understanding, and education throughout the World.

It could do that. But it requires the commitment of the People to compel their Government to make it happen.

***In 2026, there are a lot of statistics touting the prosperity of the US economy, but those numbers don't take into account that average salaries have not gone up in proportion to the rates of inflation or basic costs of living for nearly 50 years.

Further, The US Dollar remains a fiat currency. Despite assurances that tying it to a "crypto currency" means the Dollar is secure, we have already seen multiple instances where a crypto currency is only as valuable as it is agreed to be. Should those vested entities decide it is no longer in their interest to support the Dollar, it makes no difference if it's fiat or crypto, it can and will be rendered worthless.

They know this.

DAMAGE ASSESSMENTS
& DOMESTIC POLICY REFORMS

As we enter 2019 (now 2026), the United States continues to suffer under the policies and pretenses of an illegitimate government that has been functioning since W. was gifted the office in 2000. Almost none of the actions taken by the two previous administrations benefitted the Citizens of the U.S. without benefiting Corporations first. Even the vaunted "Affordable Health Care Act (Obamacare)" included a burdensome tax in violation of the 8th Amendment - penalizing Citizens who already cannot afford Health Insurance by taxing them is an excessive fine & a cruel punishment (fortunately, this has been amended, but coverage remains a requirement).

So, how to end this incestuous relationship between major Corporations and our Government? By removing and restricting their access to our Representatives through radical systemic changes which include new Amendments to our Constitution.

There are three essential steps to accomplishing this task:

1 - Repeal, Rescind & Remove all that was done before.

Since the year 2000, our Legislative Branch helped to enable and perpetuate an illegal war, passed laws and created bureaucracies that restricted U.S. Citizens in violation of the Constitution, passed laws enabling Corporate Favoritism, and refused to carry out their Constitutional responsibilities resulting in - amongst other things - manipulating nominee selections to the Supreme Court.

Simultaneously during this period, the Judicial Branch seemed to be doing its utmost to undermine and remove the "Inalienable" Rights ensured by our Constitution, allowing Corporations the ability to take land from private Citizens and influence elections, while further enabling Law Enforcement to exceed their Authority.

As the House of Representatives has clearly refused to adhere to its Constitutional obligations - those laws they swore to uphold - none of our Representatives are capable, or even worthy, of holding their office. Not only should they be fired and replaced immediately (see: Election Reforms), all laws passed during their tenure must immediately be rescinded. Any Organizations established for the purpose of subjugating Civilians (regardless of pretenses about "security") would be immediately dissolved. For example:

- The Patriot Act enabled police brutality and NSA spying: REPEALED

- The TSA, which violates the 4th and 5th Amendment daily: DISSOLVED

- The Tax on those Citizens unable to afford Health Insurance: RESCINDED

As the Supreme Court already invalidated itself by overstepping its Authority in 2000, all decisions, including those made regarding the Constitution, would immediately have to be rescinded. For example:

- Eminent Domain Decision: OVERTURNED

- Warrantless Strip Searches Decision: OVERTURNED

- Warrantless Stop & Searches Decision: OVERTURNED

To accomplish this transition back to a more Representative Democracy, there are a few "reassignments" in the duties and responsibilities of certain Government Offices which need to occur to facilitate our understanding of what was done, and what needs to be done to fix it. Specifically:

- The Government Accounting Office, The IRS, and the Department of Justice would be assigned to conduct Audits and Investigations of all Representatives from 2000 – 2019 (read: current year) for financial misconduct, selling political influence and potential Treason. These investigations would also apply to those Business Owners and Corporations that directly benefitted from conducting the illegal "War on Terror", with the intention of seizing assets, ending illegal business practices, and prosecuting those responsible for facilitating War Crimes.

- The newly reformed Legislative Branch would no longer be focused on creating and passing new Laws. Instead, it would be obligated to review all Laws and Actions over the past (26) years for Constitutional Legality, as well as oversee the many investigations both internal and external to generate a true "State of the Union Report" to U.S. Citizens within their first year, and spend the remaining years of their term engaged with the public, fixing the problems created over the past (26) years of corruption.

- All Supreme Court case decisions would have to be reviewed by a Constitutional Advisory Committee to ensure the Court adhered to its Constitutional responsibilities and was not manipulated in deciding the cases brought before the Court.

- Any Supreme Court Justice with a record of voting to "interpret" the Constitution in a way that violated the Rights of the People would be subject to censure and possible replacement.

- U.S. Citizens who were exploited by these "interpretations" of our Constitution would be allowed to seek legal recourse and just compensation from those individuals, businesses, or organizations that profited over the well being of the People.

- In an effort to streamline Federal Budgets, each Branch of Government would be subject to immediate salary review, including rescinding all raises voted for themselves since 2000.

The lifetime "golden parachute" package would be replaced with a package commiserate to the standard Federal Health Care System Insurance Policies available during their time of service.

- All Government Branch Representatives, Staff, and the private Business Owners, Lobbyists, and Corporations with whom they conducted business, would be subject to an immediate audit by the IRS and the Government Accounting Office, with referrals to law enforcement departments when appropriate.

Representatives who are cleared of impropriety would be allowed to remain in their position to the end of their term, after which, they would be replaced accordingly (see: Election Reforms).

- Those found guilty of buying and selling political influence during their time in office would be automatically subject to prosecution by the Department of Justice appropriate to the level of their crimes. In certain special circumstances, extradition opportunities for specific Individuals may be made available to certain countries depending on the nature of the accusation(s).

"But it'll never work!" Not with that attitude it won't. And why shouldn't it? It's totally non-violent, and all totally legal under our Constitution. It's our Right as U.S. Citizens to demand better from our Representatives - and we don't have to wait for an election year to do it. The very same justification for such scrutiny will be presented to them: "If you've done nothing wrong, you have nothing to fear".

Unless you prefer having these Cowards who continue to sell your Rights to Corporations keep hiding from you until they can retire with a "golden parachute"? Just because a lot of people who have been getting fat and rich off of our ignorance would suddenly lose their jobs, or their parasitic revenue streams, is that really a bad thing? Some of these same people refused to provide health care or a living wage, telling their workers to apply for welfare, simultaneously screwing over Citizens and the

Government for their own personal profit. And our "elected Representatives" helped make it happen.

Fuck all of those "Representatives" who abandoned their Duty for profit. We the People deserve better. We should demand better.

2 - Removing Corporate Influence over Government.

Billionaires are happy to give advice about how Citizens should live, and what they should do about our government, and their advice is given weight because, well, they're Billionaires - they must know something, right? Yes, they do know something. They know how to acquire and maintain their fortunes at the expense and long-term detriment of others. Not only does exorbitant wealth have undue influence over governments and politicians, it is a direct threat to the principles of Democracy.

Our Representatives have only one responsibility: to listen to the needs of their Constituency. Everything they do after that should be to fulfill those needs to the greatest benefit of the Majority. This is not to say that Business Owners do not have the right to representation, rather, it is specifically intended to clarify that no Business or Organization should have any more influence or priority above any Citizen, and that this privileged access enjoyed for so many years by such prominent figures would have to be severely restricted and enforced moving forward.

By making the election process a Federal System with Civilian Oversight, Corporations lose their ability to select the Candidates they would have in place despite the Will of the People. They become incapable of "buying" elections. In the same manner, by restricting access to our Representatives, and limiting the ability to "Lobby" (i.e. Bribe) them, we create a dynamic in government that does not depend on fundraising. There would be no need for a Representative to raise money, so no need to accept "campaign contributions".

The contained system would have no need to court Billionaire "Sponsors", and in fact, such sponsorship would only create more scrutiny regarding that Representative's intentions once in office: Why accept unnecessary money unless you were accepting a bribe...?

As a result, Representatives would also gain much more time to engage with Constituents and actually do their job as intended. Our Democratic Republic could return its focus to truly serving the Will of the People.

The Amendments proposed earlier (see: Amendments #28 & #29 in Election Reforms) would restrict Corporate Lobbying and Investment during any political campaign cycle. The following Amendments would not only restrict access to Representatives from Corporate Lobbyists, they would require open reporting of what those Lobbyists wanted and what they offered to "influence" the Representative in return:

Amendment #31: The House of Representatives shall provide equal time to all U.S. Citizens of their Constituency for matters of State and Federal Policy. Any policy concerns coming from the private sector related to Businesses, Corporations, Organizations, or large Groups need to be presented by either the individual Owner of said Business or Corporation, or a designated Representative ("Lobbyist"). Only one person shall represent said Business, Corporation, Organization, or large Group during the course of any such meeting, and all details of said meeting shall be recorded and made available to the Public immediately afterwards. As the House of Representatives is intended to represent the Will of the People, U.S. Citizens will not be denied full knowledge of what is being asked of them via their Representatives.

Amendment #32: Any Individual or Corporation that conducts business at an International Level, or generates annual profits over 500Million Dollars is immediately subject to an annual audit to ensure compliance with Federal and International Trade Laws.

--

The inherent difficulties that come from meeting basic needs, including access to education and health care, should be assuaged at least somewhat by government services, if for no other reason than demonstrating a genuine commitment to the betterment of our Nation and its People. Pain and suffering should not be a "for profit" Industry.

To that end, the following Amendment would hold Individuals as well as Businesses and Organizations directly accountable for any Corporate Malfeasance or Negligence:

Amendment #33: Individuals, Organizations, and Corporations shall not engage in any form of Agreement or Transaction that requires the subjugation or exploitation of an Individual or Group, nor the establishment of burdensome surcharges or fees, nor any other cruel and unusual obligations to any U.S. Citizens that may impair their Rights and Freedoms as guaranteed by the Constitution. Nor shall any activities be conducted that result in the irreparable damage to ecosystems, animal species, or other natural environments. No service fees or charges for offered credit, goods or services shall exceed 5% of the mutually agreed cost in question.

Amendment #34: Funding for the Social Security Program shall not be infringed upon or re-allocated for any reason. Before any such actions could be considered, Representatives would be required to initiate pay cuts to their own salaries and benefits.

The following proposals are not intended to be malicious. They are intended to help the World become a better place using Federal regulations to enforce a more compassionate approach to wealth distribution. These are just some ideas - I am sure there are more.

Global Financial Responsibility Act

-Any Individual or Business earning more than $1Billion annually would be subject to a 50% tax on income. It's not as high as the 70% tax that helped make America great in the 1950s, but it would allow for a redistribution of wealth and still allow the greedy people to keep more wealth and resources than they or their families will ever need.

-Move to seize all known assets of Individuals and Businesses attempting to hide overseas accounts and resources from taxation or review. Honesty and transparency in all things is the goal. If they hide it, they're no better than any other criminal and those resources can be put to better use saving lives, feeding and sheltering those with genuine need.

-A Global Registry, accessible to the public, of all Corporations, their Owners, their Subsidiaries, and their activities. They wouldn't have to open their books, but a clear "influence chart" detailing activities would be much more accessible for public accountability and response to any signs of criminal violations.

-End privatized Political Fundraising & Campaigning. Rallies, private events etc., are encouraged, but as Candidates would no longer be allowed to accept outside campaign contributions, fundraising would be severely restricted and conducted without candidate endorsements or exchanges for compensation or political influence.

Corporate Environmental Responsibility Act

-Move to prevent Oil Corporations from using pipelines that have been proven to leak and wreak an as yet unknown amount of environmental damage.

-Move to hold any and all Corporations accountable for all clean up and damage to eco systems occurring as a direct result from their activities.

Compassionate Corporate Responsibility Act

-Corporations with business models requiring the exploitation of Individuals or Groups, or that have a negative environmental impact, would be re-constituted to a different business model or dissolved for non-compliance.

-End privatized prisons once and for all. No U.S. Citizen should be subject to a Corporation's impression of what is "cruel and unusual" punishment. It is our Government, our Laws; therefore it should be our own Federal Institutions managing those incarcerated individuals, not "for profit" entities.

-End the privatized military (mercenaries). It is our Congress that declares War; therefore it must be our own Military that represents our Nation in combat. Specific training & education programs from private instructors would be acceptable; however, as many examples from Iraq and on could illustrate, no actual deployment for combat missions by private mercenary organizations would be allowed.

Don't like that? The Federal Government can close the entire non-compliant business and replace it with those businesses that will comply with Federal and International Law.

If Business Owners don't like these Amendments and revisions to Government Policies and Procedures, they can complain to their friends who already broke the law(s) and went to prison, or they can get out of the business entirely.

Don't like that? Well, there are a variety of psychiatric and mental illnesses that might explain the need to horde an absurd amount of wealth and natural resources to the detriment of entire populations and thousands of miles of ecosystems. Depending on the severity of the condition, those objecting Individuals could find themselves with all the amenities of wealth - food, shelter, a staff to care for them - they just wouldn't have any physical freedom as they'd be institutionalized.

And we could make all of it public record via the centralized website, so that every U.S. Citizen knew exactly who the enemy of Democracy was, and which loony bin they were locked up in where they could do no harm.

3 - De-Centralize the D.C. Power Base

Before going any further with this concept, please first consider the ease of connectivity and sharing information that we enjoy today, and how those systems are constantly refined and improved upon almost daily. Consider how relatively simple it would be to utilize current and pre-existing networks to facilitate the following proposals. Consider how the recent focus on National Security & Government Servers has already prompted investment in "unhackable" tech and unbreakable encryptions. And finally, consider how wonderful it would be to accomplish this final masterstroke against the centralized Hub of the Corporate Oligarchy known as Washington D.C.

Since 1790, the power base of the United States political system has been centralized in the D.C. Beltway. This is by Writ from the Constitution (Article I, Section 8, Clause 17). In fact, of all parts of the Constitution, this is one of a very few areas that I do feel are "quaint" and in need of updating.

All three Branches of Government are located there in D.C. Major political parties, think tanks, and lobbyist organizations are also there. And, unfortunately, after so many years of centralized power, there seems to be a profound arrogance and lack of concern for the principles this nation was founded upon emanating from there.

So, it is time to take advantage of our communication technology, utilize and adapt the resources already available, and separate the three Branches of Government to designated "Federal Hubs" across the United States. The Executive, Legislative, and Judicial Branches of Government will have to be removed from their familiar Dens of Iniquity. No more "hanging with friends" that are bad influences on their decision making ability. No more pretenses about where the money comes from, or who has authority to do what - our Constitution is the Law of the Land. The only people that seem to have a problem with it these days are the politicians "representing" us.

Time to break up the block party. Place them in parts of the country where there is no entrenched political machine, no particularly dense religious community, no lobbyists or think tanks - maybe Arkansas, Iowa and Wyoming, for example - only law abiding U.S. Citizens who want to help the government recover from its addictions and practice its newer, healthier policies and procedures. Separated from slush funds and golden parachutes, our Representatives would be required to remember the principles of ethics and Humanity that inspired and created our Constitution.

They don't have to be mutually exclusive either - certainly, having Representatives of each Branch available to liaise at each Hub would be beneficial, but the point would be to minimize the "secret negotiations" and "backroom deals", the "privileged access to power" we always hear so much about. It would impose more transparency in communication simply because Representatives would be required to communicate using Federal devices and in a manner that would be relatively simple to monitor. Booking a golf game to discuss policy with five different Lobbyists and the Executive of some poll generating Media Company wouldn't be so easy to accomplish without the public knowing of it.

If you're still not convinced, consider what happened to the Pentagon on 9/11. Imagine if - god forbid - some psycho were able to attach a Nuke to that plane - it wouldn't have been just one wall of the Pentagon, it would have been all three Branches of Government blown to shit and irradiated for thousands of years.

Separate the Branches across the Country and the success of any coordinated attack drops to near zero.

In this Information Age, communication between Branches would be relatively simple and easy to monitor. Citizens would have immediate access to Representatives via streaming chat rooms and other easy to establish, secure & maintain digital media (e.g. a centralized website). In so doing, U.S. Citizens would finally have what the Government has had on them for over a decade: an integrated, accessible database of all of our Representatives, their activities and expenditures, their travels, and - most importantly - who they met with when and regarding what subject.

The guise of "National Security" would only be applied to those activities with Foreign Nations or Allies where information critical to that sovereign nation's security may be compromised. In all other cases, the transparency of Government and the requirement of accountability would not be hindered for any reason.

SIMPLE SOLUTIONS FOR TRANSITIONING AWAY FROM THE "WAR ON TERROR" THAT WILL NEVER HAPPEN BECAUSE THERE'S NO PROFIT IN IT:

First and foremost, as Congress never formally declared war on any country in its current pursuit of the "War on Terror", all funding for this illegal, horrific, ongoing Atrocity must stop. Soldiers overseas could begin a tactical, scaled withdrawal, being re-deployed to recover U.S. Oil Facilities, resources and equipment that would ultimately have to come under the jurisdiction of the U.S. Government. After seizure, inventory & audit, U.S. Citizens could be given a genuine assessment of what was going on and who was responsible so that proper reparations could be made, paid for by these Perpetrators.

Second - All privatized military organizations and operations - the overpaid Mercenaries in particular - would have to immediately cease activities, have their assets seized, and all intelligence information reviewed for potential war crimes prosecution. All "private industry" personnel would be required to return to the United States and interview with Federal Officials regarding their activities. Any failure to appear would automatically make any private industry Owner, Operator or Personnel a Fugitive from Justice.

Finally - Those Private Companies directly involved in the planning, invasion, and illegal occupation that became known as the "War on Terror" would have to be seized, the Executives investigated for possible arrest on charges of fraud, treason, and violations under the RICO Act. Once arrested and assets seized, investigations would spread outward to those affiliates and allies who knowingly facilitated these war crimes.

Simply by divesting from the "War on Terror" and seizing the assets of those companies & the (alleged) War Criminals that ran them, the United States gains trillions of Dollars in liquid cash and assets on top of the renewed respect of our Allies, and an opportunity to continue trading under new economic models, leading to a healthy infrastructure and robust International trade. It's better than our current path of exploitation and murder.

But then, what "tangible goods" do we tie our Dollar to so that it can remain competitive?

Why not go back to a Gold Standard...? Russia and China are already doing it. If estimates are correct, we still possess the most gold and therefore could control that market as well, so what are we worried about...?

Big Oil has no new ideas beyond more poisonous destruction. We need a new Industry, and real economic stability that a Military backed, Oil-based economy simply cannot provide. After nearly twenty years, we've seen the results and know that Fossil Fuels are unsustainable in every sense of the term.

We need to get smart and get out before the rest of the world makes us do it.

RESTORING THE FOCUS
OF LOCAL LAW ENFORCEMENT

We do not need a militarized Police Force. That is why we have the National Guard. The practice of training local law enforcement to view every encounter as a possible "terrorist threat" undermines the purpose of a Civilian Police Force, which is simply to ensure the safety of their Community. The most successful Law Enforcement encounters begin with an attitude of respect and service rather than demanding submission to the Badge. Any training encouraging belligerent tactics only exacerbates a potentially volatile situation.

Further, the aggressive "us vs. them" training leads to abuse of authority, violence, death, and in the case of North Dakota specifically, it has led to State Police acting as mercenaries in defiance of their sworn oaths of Office. For a Civilian population to fear its local Police Department should be unacceptable in a Free Society. This fear of Police abusing their authority must be addressed by a review and revision of training procedures.

THE VETS, UNEMPLOYED, HOMELESS, & FOSTER CARE

A Nation that abandons its own Citizens is not worthy of being called a Democracy. The fact that our nation has a manufactured disparity of wealth also means that disparity can be corrected. With the reduction in military spending, a re-allocation of resources would allow for funding education and support programs designed to address some of the issues related to our homeless and children in foster care - specifically in terms of providing comfortable, safe home environments, proper educational resources, and a counseling system that helps ensure job placement and future development for those Young Adults transitioning out of Foster Care.

The fact that any U.S. Citizen should be neglected, or prevented from fulfilling their pursuit of Liberty and Happiness by their own Government, should be unacceptable in a civilized Society.

For Veterans of Military Service:

Amendment #35: Congress shall not conduct any activities related to War without first ensuring that there is a sufficient allocation of resources to provide proper munitions and armor, as well as proper medical care and any other resources necessary for those Soldiers and Civilians wounded in service to their Country.

No Representative in any Branch of Government shall have a Health Insurance or "Benefits" Plan that exceeds what is provided to our retired Veterans and Service Personnel.

ILLEGAL IMMIGRATION REFORMS

With a seated President sending Soldiers to "protect our Borders" from a dubious caravan of "Illegal Invaders", actively separating children from family members only to somehow "lose them" in the beleaguered bureaucracy of foster care, while at the same time enabling and employing the very same types of vilified "Undocumented Workers" to clean and cook in his very own Resort Hotels, Trump could not better exemplify the most despicable form of Hypocrite in America today. (And that was written in 2016!)

The situation is very simple: Businesses have built an Industry dependent upon exploiting illegal immigrants seeking a better life in the United States than they were living elsewhere. The fact that these "Home Nations" do not elevate their own Citizens, or even further, that our own Government does not help these other Nations to build better care and services for their own Citizens, is proof that there is no real intention to change the situation on either side of the border. And here is Trump caught playing both ends against the middle for as much profit as he and his cronies can squeeze before being stopped.

This is another deliberate failure on the part of our Government, choosing to protect Corporate Interests at the expense of its own Citizens, and the Citizens of other Nations. This failure could be easily rectified; not only by enforcing our own laws, but also by helping other nations elevate their own economy and ability to care for their own Citizens.

From this first step, investigations, audits, and arrests of Businesses, Business Owners, and Individuals who defied Federal Law to exploit Human Beings as cheap labor would ensue, sending a clear message that such abuses would no longer be tolerated. The Labor Force would also be encouraged to form Unions, where they could negotiate for proper pay, health care, and whatever on site resources necessary and useful for the safe completion of their work.

The only stipulation related to Citizenship would be:

Any and All People living within the United States are subject to the Laws of the Land, same as any other Citizen. No other Nation's Law, No Religious Law, No personal Code of Ethics supersedes the Constitution or U.S. Laws.

This could be tacked on as a "Rider" to any new law or proposed amendment Congress is attempting to pass right now. Pretty simple.

Don't like that? Get escorted out with no invitation to return.

In this manner, we do not provide Amnesty, but we do take down a brutal Criminal Industry, gain Legal Residents and newly "Documented" Immigrants & Migrant Workers who are able to contribute to the United States as any other person with a work permit, visa, or earned Citizenship - without fear, without being exploited, without having to hide, without having to worry what will happen to their children.

The only people preventing a sensible resolution to this problem are the Business Owners and Lawyers who continue to profit from this perpetual exploitation and strife.

They must be held accountable.

MORE POLICIES, PROGRAMS & OTHER GOOD IDEAS

Prior to becoming a Corporate Oligarchy, the United States was effectively a Capitalist Republic. Neither was good for Democracy. Both function based on the Imperialist perspective that one group must be subjugated by another for Government to function properly - or something like that. For profit to be made, it must be taken from someone or somewhere. There is nothing wrong with commerce, earning a living, or even living well; however, in a Democratic, "Civilized" Society, such extreme disparity of wealth, abuse of Labor & Citizens and exploitation of Natural Resources would not exist. It would not exist simply because "average" Citizens would not allow it to exist.

For (26) years, we have been fast tracked, moved further and further away from the Ideologies and Intentions of our Founding Fathers. What follows are more ideas regarding Amendments, Acts, Policies & Programs which become easily affordable and actionable by simply ending this criminal "war on an emotion", compelling Corporations to pay their taxes & act responsibly, and encouraging diligent Citizenship to prevent this situation from ever happening again...

-Whistleblower Protection Program: Any information leading to the prosecution of Government or Corporate Crimes will automatically receive protections from prosecution or retribution and in most cases receive rewards based on the nature of the information provided. Bring Edward Snowden Home, with Honors, as a start.

- Citizen's Investigation & Information Verification Commission: Forget about Wikipedia, Snopes, and all those other unvetted, unverified, online "verification sources". One centralized database with confirmed facts, news source interviews & confirmations administered by Librarians & academics with no vested interest in the information or how it is presented beyond being factual and accurate.

- Repeal The 16th Amendment - This Amendment was introduced to help pay for the War at that time. That war is long since over, and the budget is bloated beyond necessity. Cutting military spending in half would make taxing employee's wages no longer necessary, and therefore the practice should be ended.

- Dissolve The Two-Party System - This political device deliberately keeps Citizens divided, misinformed, and incapable of receiving proper Representation in Government. Its Leaders would be investigated and prosecuted for violations under the RICO Act.

- Rescind Common Core - end the ridiculous, deliberate dumbing down of our Citizenry. Base new education programs on successful International Education Models.

- End Student Loan Debts Immediately - return to educational grants and scholarship programs.

- Provide Training & Education Programs - particularly for those former employees of disbanded Federal & Federally funded Organizations to assist in the transition to alternate career paths in government or private sector fields.

- Develop Alternative Energy Programs - The separation of the United States from dependence on Oil is critical to the advancement of our Society as a whole.

- Legalize Hemp In All Forms - immediately begin researching Industrial, Medicinal & Clinical applications for immediate implementation.

- End GMOs & Chemical Spraying - Fuck Monsanto and their "Poison for Profit" ilk into the Earth.

- Prevent Farmers From Plowing Crops Under To Control Pricing - any extra bulk food supplies would be redistributed and donated to Homeless Shelters, and/or exported to starving Nations. The fact that our Nation chooses to destroy food to control profits instead of feeding starving Families anywhere in the World – even their own neighbors next door - is a crime against Humanity, and must stop immediately.

- Move To A Federal Health Care Program - a real one, fully funded, no co-pay bullshit, no penalty taxes, no "surprise" increase in payments. Insurance Companies restricted to covering Cars, Homes, Disasters & Luxury Items.

- Move To Develop Alternative Health Programs - The refusal on the part of Big Pharma to explore natural cures is indicative of a "Profit over People" mentality; therefore, in addition to the Investigations already mentioned, Government subsidies will be re-directed into the exploration of Alternative Medicines and Natural Therapies with the specific intention of maintaining affordable solutions to an informed & healthy Citizenry.

- Cap All Pharmaceutical Drugs Pricing At No More Than 20% Above Production Costs - Any more profit on Human suffering is simply cruel.

- Review All Credit Cases Related To Health Care - including "pre-existing disabilities" and mental health care coverage with the intention of absolving debt and providing necessary access to treatment and care as determined by the patient and caregiver, not an outside third party.

All of this is possible, totally legal under our Constitution, and would elevate our Culture and Society without undermining any Individual Rights or Freedoms. The only segment of our Society that would suffer are those Corporations and Owners of said Corporations that have spent at least (26) years plotting and maneuvering to remove your Rights and Freedoms, so that they could extract as much material wealth as possible while steering this country down a horrific policy of engaging in Illegal Wars for Profit.

All of this must end. But it takes more than the Will of the People to make it happen. It takes Love, Hope & Patriotism. Without that, the Constitution truly is "quaint", and America truly is Dead.

LAST WORDS (Revised)

"Committing Patriotism" was extracted and revised from my previous book "America's Dead and You're Next". The section it comes from, "It'll Never Happen, But..." was presented in a bit more cynical manner to match the motif, but the fact is, these are viable solutions to today's political problems - not the only ones, of course, but none of these solutions require violence to accomplish their goals.

 I do not expect this book to be revolutionary or change the world. What I do expect is that, by compiling my own notes & observations, I can offer something to those who may have gone, or are currently going through a similar journey, and may be trying to do something about what they see happening around them. Even if that something is writing a book like this one.

There is enormous Freedom in letting go of anything that you are not directly responsible for - and anything that you are responsible for should be tied directly to one simple question: How does it help? If it causes more harm than good - especially over the long run - maybe consider another path.

Helping others is a direct path to achieving your own personal Happiness. We know this. And yet, we find ourselves inundated with information designed to frighten us, teaching us to practice the opposite of kindness - to be suspicious instead of compassionate, and to accept that Hatred must be matched by more Hatred.

So, for my part, I step down from this platform of clamoring over calamity. I am invigorated by the sudden multitude of voices that have spoken up, asking questions and demanding answers. Perhaps what I see as inevitable is merely a myopic interpretation of limited information. Perhaps the information in this book will be useful to others.

I do believe that access to information and the ability to communicate will serve coming generations far better than it served any before, so there is Hope.

There is always Hope.

In the meantime, I am responsible for my own bills, my own family, and my own income to maintain the standard of living to which I have become accustomed, same as the rest of us. Saying farewell to the Anger was the healthiest thing I could do, and I encourage others to do the same.

For, as this Journal reveals, Fear, Anger, Outrage, Indignation - all natural responses, yes - but, all of these aggressive emotions have a cost. And that cost is your own well-being - your Spirit, your Soul, your Humanity.

Choose Happiness. Help others. Take care of your own. That's the best you can do - and will be able to do - in these Interesting Times ahead of us.

 Love to All.

***--> This was originally written somewhere around 2014 – 2016, extracted and re-published in 2019. And reviewed & revised again in January, 2026.

- For this most recent update, some corrections are noted with a parenthesis, as when I mention the year, instead of 2019, it will read (2026) – e.g. I wrote this (26) years ago.

- There are also asterisks (***) noting where there is as update to the subject matter at the end of the chapter.

ABOUT THE AUTHOR

Brad Havens is not a politician or a soldier. His opinions are speculation at best, based on conclusions drawn from a variety of resources, some of which have been simultaneously confirmed and denied, depending on the "verification organization" reviewing specific information made available to the public.

All subjective conclusions have been researched, reviewed and presented based on the majority of circumstantial information available via Public Library or Internet resources - there are no conclusions based solely on a singular statement by one unverified source. In other words, years of Independent research went into these conclusions, there are no "a guy in a bar told me once..." opinions presented here.

Born in Michigan to a family of Educators & Health Care Professionals, Brad was immediately drawn to movies and story telling, and the desire to do that for a living instead of following in any more traditional familial profession. His Family's interest in politics, however, was attractive to him - deeply rooted in Love of Country and Constitution - and on many an evening, the Family's Sunday gathering for dinner would end up in a round table discussion of what was happening in the world, and what our government was doing about it.

They were lively and fun conversations, and people could be equally upheld or derided for their opinions, because the point was to examine, discuss, and determine what was right - not to submit to one thought alone as being correct, but to hear other's opinions and weigh them for their merit before deciding what was best for the person. Dissent was necessary for good political conversation in this Family.

And so the calling to make movies took him away from the familiar, and off to the magical world of California, where his interest in politics abated somewhat until that fateful day on 9/11/2001, when the course of Human History changed forever. To this day, seeing 9/11 anywhere - even just telling the time -

invokes an instinctive shudder at the thought of the horrific tragedy of all that was lost on that day.

Since that day, and then over the following several years, sanity was lost and recovered as Ideologies were shattered and re-formed. A new paradigm view of the World and how it operated was re-shaped and re-formed over years of inquiry and research.

This book is the culmination of those years.

No longer angry, no longer outraged, this Journal is released as the last epilogue from all of that. Perhaps this treatise will help other U.S. Citizens, or anybody anywhere who may be experiencing their own deep rooted Ideologies and World View shaken by recent events, come to a peace within themselves much quicker than it took the Author to do so himself.

THANKS FOR THE HELP!

My parents, for becoming compass points to keep my bearings while navigating a nearly blinding storm. Thank you.

My brother, for being there when I landed. Thank you

Shannon, a million "Thank Yous" will never be enough. Here's another one: Thank you!

Shaun, for being Brave, taking the Leap, & making Magic happen - Thank you!

Every other person who heard my voice and did not run & hide. Thank you.

www.MountainFireMedia.com

www.ingramcontent.com/pod-product-compliance
Lightning Source LLC
Chambersburg PA
CBHW051422250726
48655CB00003B/1194